Mother Pearl Book of Poetry

Tommie Pearl Holmes

ISBN-10: 0615450083
ISBN-13: 978-0615450087 (Henry G.\Holmes)

LCCN:

DEDICATION

This is the day the Lord was made; I hope all is well and Rejoicing in it. I am Tommie Pearl Holmes. I was born in Cataula, Ga. On December Twenty-fifth, Nineteen Hundred Twenty, to Janie Iola and Jacob Ward. My family moved to Columbus Ga. when I was three years old. I went to Fifth Ave Grade School. I started there in the second grade because my mother who was a supply teacher taught me at home. I also had two aunts who were teachers.

I attended Spencer Vocational High School in Columbus, Ga., where I majored in Home Economics and Nursing. I also attended Jamaica Vocational High School of Jamaica, New York, where I continued my training for Practical Nursing.

One of my aunts was the Principal of East Highland High School. I had many talented helpful members in my family who taught me and helped me along, by editing my writing and encouraging me to take up writing seriously. The rest is HISTORY.

I worked six years for the state and nine years for The City Of New York, and also eighteen years at Star Registry for Nurses in Brooklyn, New York.

I was a member of Jackson Memorial AMEZ Church. I transferred from Jackson to Calvary AMEZ Church in Jamaica, New York, because it was more convenient for me to reach.

My present Pastor is Reverend Dr. E. Alex Brower of Calvary.

CONTENTS

CONTENTS

CONTENTS

ACKNOWLEDGMENTS

It is good to be able to share some of my past experiences. I was born December 25, 1920. I used to sing with a group called Heaven Bound. We would sing on Sunday mornings on the air (WRRL) Radio Station. I also want to share and thank God for the gift of writing. I certainly do enjoy writing and I surely do know that he has ways of speaking to his people, especially the ones that he has put his Spirit upon. At one time though the Holy Spirit, he spoke to me saying "I give you these words to give to my people". I certainly know that a lot of my inspiration comes from having such a beautiful church family. At the are of 7 years old I came to Christ. My church home was St. John's African Methodist Church in Columbus, Georgia. I have been blessed. I have met many beautiful people. A lot of them became my friend and up to this date are still my friends. Through all of these friends, I had a lot of beautiful memories. I was a member of Jackson Memorial African Methodist Episcopal Zion Church in Hempstead, Long Island, New York from 1962 to 1969. However, due to incontinence in transportation, I got a transfer to my present church, Calvary African Methodist Episcopal Zion Church in Jamaica, New York in 1969. I came to Calvary and joined. My past pastor from Jackson Memorial AMEZ Church, Rev.

Sinclair sent a very nice recommendation letter to Calvary AME Zion Church to Pastor Dennis Hogan. I have been serving as a consecrated Deaconess to date.

I have lived in New York since the age of 23. Through many of these beautiful moments, there is one that I will always cherish. Because of having such beautiful people as my church family, namely Calvary AME Zion Church family, I met my beautiful husband Henry Madison Holmes. I thank God for the years that we had together. Him being a beautiful artist and me being a writer knitted us together as one. Our marriage grew stronger as our love has remained.

1 A MAN'S PRAYER

My heavenly father

As I sit here in the quiet of my room

I know that you know my heart

You know all about me

The words before I say them

My Lord

It is so wonderful to serve Thee!

The one that made me

Why wouldn't I come to you?

My Lord in prayer

I know that you are a just God

A God of understanding

A God of hope and charity

Help me my Lord to be more like Thee

I am grateful my father

For the blessed life has been given me

Sometimes the mountains of life are high

Sometimes I did not understand

Sometimes the roads are rough and long

And it seemed things were all wrong

I know my Lord the rivers of life are deep

And I know oh Lord by your holy words

You will never leave me alone

With that assurance I know Lord

You will be there when I cross

The River Of Life

To take my hand

Amen

By: Pearl T. Holmes

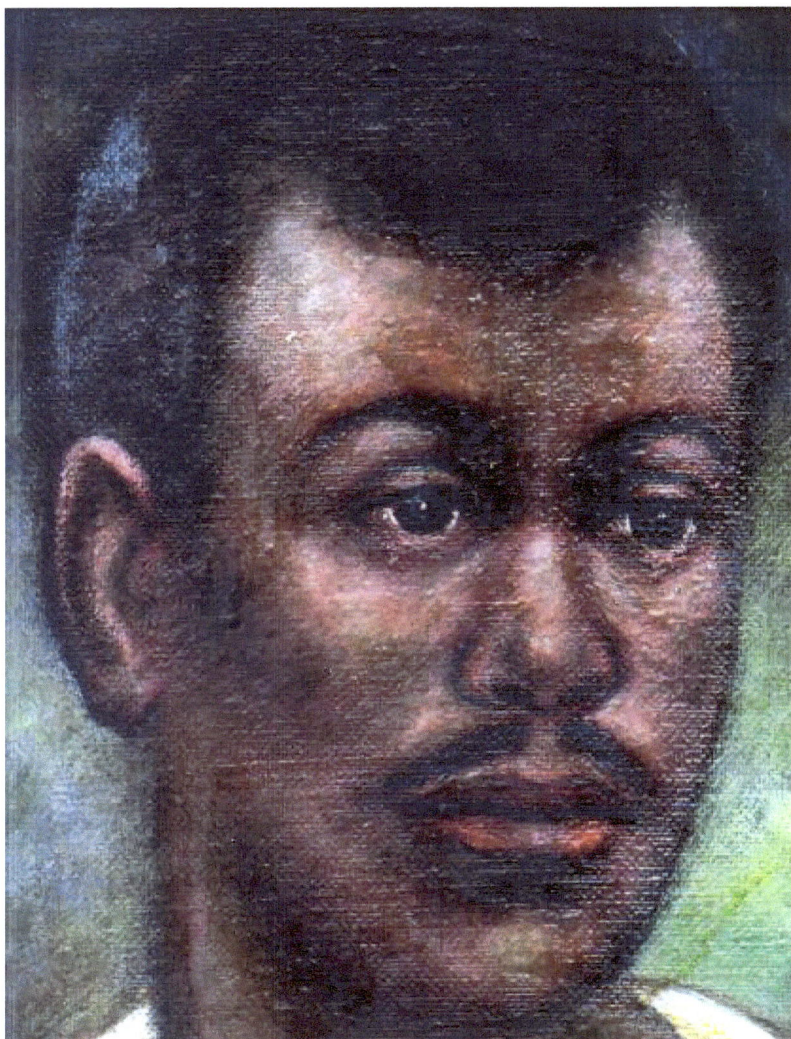

2 CHARITY IN PRAYER

Do you really love the Lord? I really love the Lord!

As I grow older I often think to myself what have I done with the summer days? Vacation time? Now it is fall; and winter is on its way. Just where did all those hours and days go. There are people I didn't see at all over the summer.

I want to say to you, let us share the Lord. I am going to ask you to set aside a few minutes a day at the same time to pray with me, for each other. For God, all time stands still, so it doesn't matter if we are in a different place, God can put us at Jesus' feet together in prayer.

Friends share that is the first lesson as a child,
I was taught, as Christians, you not only share
what you have, but also share what you are.
Example of charity, a trusting, faithful, joyful
servant of God, freely you have received, freely
give.

Do you really love the Lord? Then let us
share him.

By: Pearl Holmes

Tommy Pearl Holmes

3 CHRIST

He walked the earth, just as you and me,

He was born in Bethlehem across the sea,

He wore no shoes, he held no school degree,

He died, humbly on a tree to set man free.

It is not enough for us, to sit on a high stand and
say I love thee.

Let us make a joyful noise in this land,

Let your love shine from your country to mine;

Let us connect the Holy line around the world
sublime!

And cling together, like clinging vines.

Christ came to save, Mankind!

By: Pearl Holmes

4 GOD'S GIFT

God's gift to me: Life, Love, Faith,
understanding wisdom, dominion, peace, poise,
power, health, enthusiasm, abundance,
friendship, courage, perseverance, choice,
strength, forgiveness, vitality, joy, justice,
harmony, order, imagination, divinity, light,
confidence, balance, patience, success, and
freedom.

I am filed with the fullness of God.
I give and receive from an Infinite source.
I am an expression of the Infinite.
As I let it live through me,
All problems are dissolved.

By: Pearl Holmes

5 HAPPY LITTLE BLUEBIRD

Somewhere over the rainbow, well up high,
happy little bluebird fly, Bird fly over the
rainbow and why o why can't you and I.
Somewhere over the rainbow there is a land that
I dream of, one in a lull-li-by happy little
bluebird fly. O tell me, O tell me then, then why
can't you and I.

By: Tommie Pearl Holmes

6 HAPPY VALENTINE

Long as the vine grow around the stump,

And the grape grow in bunches,

You are my valentine,

And I am your sugar lump,

Happy Valentine day.

By: Tommie Pearl Holmes

7 HIS LOVE

All of the honey from the honey bees,
All of the sugar from the maple trees;
Wouldn't be as sweet
As God's love for me.

All of the rubies,
And diamonds that sparkle radiantly,
All the pearls from the deep sea,
Wouldn't be as pure and precious as
His love for me!

It is the oldest story that has been told,
God doesn't want your riches and gold;
He will give you his love, for your soul!

By: T. Pearl Holmes

8 I AM TIRED OF EVERYTHING BUT YOU

I am tired of the subway line trying to reach

my job to punch the time clock by nine.

I'm tired of the lunch bell chime, it seems I'm

working hard all the time.

I cannot get you off my mind.

Yeah, Yeah, Yeah, Yeah!!

I'm tired of lonely walk in the park,

Hoping I will find you sitting there in the dark,

as well as I carry you around in my heart.

Oh how I wish it would come true, I am tired

of everything but you.

Yeah, Yeah, Yeah, Yeah!!!

Tommy Pearl Holmes

I'm tired of the four walls in my room waiting
for a call saying you will be coming soon.
Yet, I'm sitting here crying my heart out getting
tired of feeling blue and missing you.
O how I wish it would come true, I'm tired of
everything but you.
Yeah, Yeah, Yeah, Yeah!!!!

By: T. Pearl Holmes

9 I WANT TO SING MERRY CHRISTMAS TO YOU

I want to sing Merry Christmas to you

I know you will be singing the same to me

This is the season to be happy

So let us dance around the Christmas tree.

So let us dance around the Christmas tree

This is the season to be happy

Let us dance around the Christmas tree.

I want to sing Merry Christmas to our great

country

And to all the lands across the sea

Hoping someday they will all agree and be

free.

So let us dance around the Christmas tree

Hoping they will all be free

So let us dance around the Christmas tree.

By: T. Pearl Holmes

10 IT'S A BEAUTIFUL DAY

#1 It is a blessed time of the day to bring the gospel your way, just call God's line, he's never too busy to listen to what you have to say, HALLELUJAH!!! He knows all about your sorrow and will never turn you away.

It is a beautiful day to pray………
It is a beautiful, wonderful time to pray
OOOOOO!

#2 It is a glorious time of the day for all mankind to stop, kneel and pray. Just open your mouth, he will supply the words for you to say. Praise his name! Why not let him have his way!

It is a beautiful day to pray………

It is a beautiful, wonderful time to pray

OOOOOO!

By: T. Pearl Holmes

11 LET EVERYTHING WITH BREATH PRAISE THE LORD

I thank you Lord for the little happy birds that sings.

I thank you Lord for the bright sunshine and the Holy rain, Oh----I thank you Lord for all the joy and peace that you bring…

Let everything with breath praise his name

Let everything with breath praise his holy name!

Let all of God's creation praise his name!

Let everything with breath praise his name!

I thank you Lord for bringing us over the dark and lonely lane

For giving us hope, faith, and a mind to
understand---Oh---I thank you Lord for holding
our hands.

Let everything with breath praise his name

Let everything with praise his holy name!

Let all of God's creation praise his name!!

Let everything with breath praise his name.

By: Pearl Holmes

12 LITTLE BUNGALOO

Live can mean a walk down a shady lane,

It can mean two hands when they are held tight

It can mean two pairs of eyes with love gleaming light

It can mean a white pickett fence around a bungalow, where your name and mine are on the door.

It can mean wearing out feet in the sand, by the moon peek over the water that flow,

It can mean a table set for tea at four in the little bungalow where your name and my name is on the door.

Love can mean the working sound of the sea,

It can mean how soft you voice can be,

It can mean the clock on the wall striking three, when I feel your lips with a kiss in the little bungalow where your name and my name are on the door.

Tommie Pearl Holmes

13 Love Must Be Free

Love must be as free, and bright as the sun
that sheds it's "beams on everyone",
warming all hearts, closing out the dark, as
we take this walk with God!

Love must be as free, soft and mellow as
the moon light

giving out it's rays of quietness,
tranquility;

with soothing calmness that guides us;
and we know

God's peace is with us tonight!

Love must be free, and strong as the wind
forgetting

self and world below, with eyes on
"heaven's shore"

But remembering God's children in valleys below.

Love must be free, clean and fresh as rain, that falls

on the mountains and plains, and returns to the sea

of hope again. The mighty little drops of rain

aboundly supplys our heart, "with God's gain"!

By: Pearl Holmes

14 LOVE

It is the Love of God we kneel in prayer

Remembering his Son, Christ, as he hung there,

It was love that gave God his plans

  To create the world in which he made Man.

It is the smile on your face

  That you wear each day

As you run the Christian Race.

Let us know in our hearts,

That God's love is real.

It is the love of God the let us know

He will be with us tomorrow,

As he was yesterday and today.

              By : Pearl Holmes

15 MORNING PRAYER

O'Lord, our Father, at this time of the morning

I come, My Lord to you in Prayer,

Thanking you for our night of rest

And for waking us up.

Father, if there is anything in our hearts that is not pleasing to your Commandments, we do ask forgiveness. O'God of mercy, help us to forgive each other. Give us understanding hearts with faith, trusting in thee. Teach us how to pray and what to pray for. Lord, thank you for our benefits, homes and place of worship.

We do ask your blessing for your dear people in need throughout the world.

Bless our government

Blessed is the nation whose God is the Lord and help us to make the right decisions for our people.

Please, Father, accept my humble prayer in spite of my unworthiness.

In the name of the Father, and the Son and the
Holy spirit.

Amen.

By: Pearl Holmes

16 MOTHER HOLMES ELECT PRESIDENT BARAK OBAMA AND FAMILY

Heavenly Father, I am coming to you today, to speak the things that I have in my heart and mind concerning your children. We are thankful for your beautiful blessing and things that you have given us.

We thank you for health and sound mind; you have given us a beautiful world to live in, and you have supplied all the things that you would want your children to have, and you have supplied supplied our earth earth with beautiful flowers of all colors.

You have created different denominations with different colors and just like the beautiful flowers you want them to come together in kindness and respect one for the other.

We thank you O Lord for giving us the person that was elect for President of our country for the next four years, and having connection with foreign country, we know the work is not upon the one person that is President. It is upon all nations.

We thank you for the blessing we have already received, and in our hearts and mind Dear Father, we want to come together and stand together, and continue together, in your holy and righteous name. We thank you for blessing our country, and blessing our world.

Amen

By: Mother Tommie Pearl Holmes

Jamaica, New York

December 2008

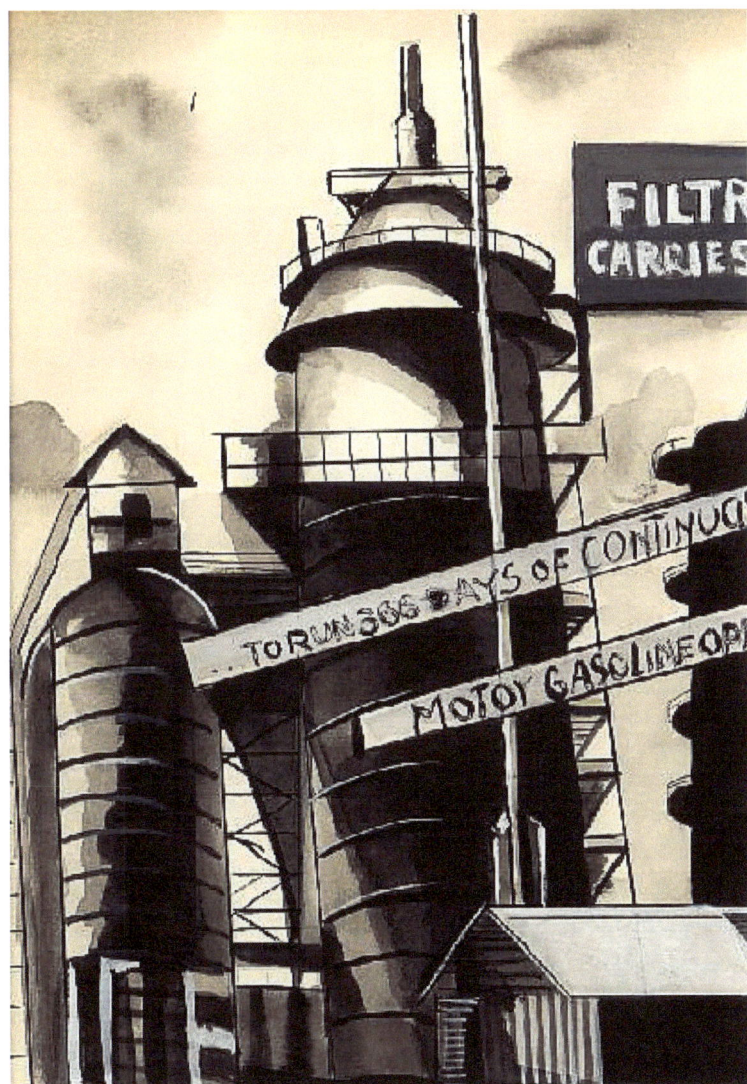

17 PILGRAM GOING HOME

Oh the rich man is high and mighty,

  Trying to stay at the top to prove that he is strong.

The poor man is carrying the weight of the world on his arms

And is just holding on,

I'm just a pilgrim going home

I'm just a pilgrim going home

I'm here to teach you love, peace and understanding in a song.

Down the glory road where no more billows will roll.

I'm just a pilgrim going home, Yes, I'm just a pilgrim going home.

We can't all sing like David

  No, we can't all preach like Paul

We can love everybody, and stand up strong and tall.

And God's grace will save us all,

Yes, I am a pilgrim going home,

I am just a pilgrim going H-o-m-e.

By: Pearl Holmes

18 RAILROAD MAN

Do not say good buy my love that will make me cry my love, just say so long my love and I be strong, my love while you are gone my love.

I won't be alone my love, I be mopping floor and working clothes doing a little shopping at the novelty store, seeing the children off to school in between missing you, in between feeling blue always loving you Saturday.

You will return home my love that will be our day along Susan wil be visiting her Aung Man, Billy will be attending his ball game, I will be back in your arm again,

Welcome home my railroad man, welcome home from the railroad game.

Welcome home my railroad man!!

By: Tommie Pearl Holmes

19 SHARING THE PAST

It is good to be able to share some of my past experiences. I was born December 25, 1920. I used to sing with a group called Heaven Bound. We would sing on Sunday mornings on the air (WRRL) Radio Station. I also want to share and Thank God for the gift of writing. I certainly do enjoy writing and I surely do know that he has ways of speaking to his people, especially the one that He has put His Spirit upon. At one time though the Holy Spirit He spoke to me saying "I give you these words to give to my people". I certainly know that a lot of my inspiration comes from having such a beautiful church family. At the age of 7 years old I came to Christ. My church home was St. John's African Methodist Church in Columbus, Georgia. I have been blessed. I have met many beautiful people. A lot of them became my friends and up to this date are still my friends. Through all of these friends, I had a lot of beautiful memories. I was a member of Jackson Memorial African Methodist Episcopal Zion Church in Hempstead from 1962 to 1969. However, due to inconvience in transportation, I got a transfer to my present church, Calvary African Methodist Episcopal Zion Church in Jamaica, New York in 1969. I came to Calvary and joined. My past pastor from Jackson Memorial AMEZ Church Reverend Sinclair sent a very nice recommendation letter to Calvary AME Zion Church to Pastor Dennis Hogan. I have been serving as a consecrated Deaconess to date.

I have lived in New York since the age of 23. Through many of these beautiful moments, there is one that I will always cherish. Because of having such beautiful people as my church family, namely Calvary AME Zion Church family, I met my beautiful husband Henry Madison Holmes. Him being a beautiful artist and me being a writer knitted us together as one. Our marriage grew stronger as our love has remained.

20 SHIP TO OUTER SPACE

I wandered off to outer space, there were sky ships sailing on the sea of Dreams,

Going around the hills of Love; and over the mountains of Faith, and into the Golden gates. There I saw a smile on each Angel's face.

On the throne of grace sat the King of Kings, The Mother of Heaven and Earth, sat Holy Mary the Queen.

As the ship sailed around the Bay of Hope, I heard glorious music on Silver tambourines

Heavenly songs were sung; Telling me, "The Rainbow was being hung". Clouds of joy that wash away all tears, No age limit, no years, time stands still.

As I drifted down to the Sea of forgetfulness to return no more,

Where the rose of Sharon and the Sweet Lillies of the valley grow;

To gather honey, to feed, until I hunger no more! A voice from the Turtle Dove said, Awake!

It is time to go back to Old Times, Old Things, Old Friends, and Old Places.

The sky ship will return!

Back to Outer Spaces.

By: Pearl T. Holmes

21 SPIRIT OF WISDOM

In the name of the Father, and the Son, and the Holy Spirit…….

Come Holy Spirit, fill the hearts of your faithful, and enkindle in them the fire of your love.

Send forth your Spirit and they shall be created and you shall renew the face of the earth.

Father, you taught the hearts of your faithful people by sending them the light of your Holy Spirit, the joy of His comfort and guidance.

We ask this through our Lord Jesus Christ, Your Son, who lives and reigns with you and the Holy Spirit and one God, for ever and ever.

Amen.

By: Pearl T. Holmes

22 THANK GOD

Thank you Dear God, for beautiful flowers growing in the vast meadow green,

Thank you for the Holy rain that makes them beam,

Thank you for the tall trees standing there, shadowing us from the Sun's magnificient glare.

Thank you for the soft white snow, that falls through Heaven's open door, reflect with the moon and stars to give out, God's silver bars the glow.

Thank you Dear God, for the little children that are happy at play and on the go.

Thank you for such a beautiful day.

Thank you Dear God, for the old people that have struggled along life's way.

Thank you for directing their hands, as they worked and toiled,

Thank you for protecting their homes, when troubles boiled;

Thank you Dear God, for letting us stay in such a beautiful land, that has yield so much, to prepare us to meet you in our home far away, when it is time to go!

By: Pearl Holmes

23 THANK YOU LORD

I thank you Lord for the little happy bird that
sing for the bright sun shine and the Holy rain,

I thank you for the joy and peace that they bring.

Let everything with breath praise your Holy
name.

I thank you Lord, when you said you would
make men and make him a mate, a woman. A
woman to walk with him through the land and
that they shall bring to this earth, woman child
and man child.

Let everything with breath praise your Holy
name.

By: Tommie Pearl Holmes

24 THE CARPENTER'S SON

He is the Prince of peace.

He is the King of Kings

He is the corner stone,

He will be with you when all your friends are gone…..

He is the Carpenter's son, his name is Jesus

Yea, his name is Jesus, His name is Je------sus

He came to get his Heavenly Father's work done.

He is the lilly of the valley

He is the Rose of Sharon

He is the good shepherd

He will leave the ninety-nine and go after the one that is lost ----------

He is the Carpenter's Son, his name is Jesus,

Yea, his name is Jesus, His name is Je-----sus

He came to get his Heavenly Father's work done.

By: Pearl Holmes

25 THE NAME OF JESUS

Stand up and bless the Lord your God forever and ever, and blessed be his glorious name,

By how many names and titles is our Saviour mentioned? Over one hundred…..

For unto us a child is born – Unto us a Son is given – and His name shall be called; "Wonderful Counselor, The Might God, The Everlasting Father, The Prince Of Peace."

God has highly exalted him and given him a name which is above every name. He is the Lord of Lords and the King of Kings, Chief among ten thousand, Son of the Living God, Lion of the tribe of Judah, The Bright and Morning Star, the Light of the World, the Good Shepherd.

Which of all his names is the sweetest? "Jesus!!!" The Precious Cornerstone, The Friend of Sinners, The Man of Sorrows.

Oh, Magnify the Lord within me, and let us exalt his name together.

Why was he called Jesus? Thou shalt call His name Jesus, For he shall save his people from their sins. Neither is there salvation in any other,

For there is none other name under the Heaven, given among men whereby we must be saved. He is the Captain of our Salvation, The Author and Finisher of our FAITH, The Head of the Church, He is The way, The Truth and The Life.

By: Pearl Holmes

26 WEDDING DAY (1974)

I want the April rain to remind you of Beautiful things, because today you Are my queen. (GROOM)

I want the sun to shine from up above and protect you. You are the boy I love. (BRIDE)

We want to search for King Solomon's Gold, and find riches, riches untold. And that we will never grow old on this Our Wedding Day. (TOGETHER)

We want the honeybee to gather nectar. From all the trees to keep our love. Sweet until eternity, on this our Wedding Day. (TOGETHER)

We want the bells to ring as the bearer marches with our rings. And the Chapel Choir to sing. (TOGETHER)

We want the rice to pour as we go through the door. And the waiting world to know, we love each other so, on this our wedding day. (TOGETHER)

By: Pearl Holmes

27 YESTERDAY SONG

YESTERDAY

BY ... PEARL HOLMES

" For The Children "

Have you watched the dawn fade a - way ---------- and the sun's beams make a new day; -------- To - mor - row is now· to-day -------- · and yes-ter-day· is now but yes-ter-day --------

(RECITATION) WILL SOMEONE REMEMBER BECAUSE YOU CAST A LOVING SMILE THEIR WAY .. OR WILL THEY REMEMBER THE LONELY SOUL YOU HELPED TO FIND HOPE AND FAITH ... DID YOU STOP TO HEAR A CRYING CHILD'S CRY TURN TO LAUGHTER AND PLAY ... DID YOU STOP TO PRAY WHEN THINGS DID NOT GO YOUR WAY?

IF YOU DID NOT MAKE SOMEONE HAPPY YESTERDAY, THERE WILL ALWAYS BE TOMORROW .. IF YOU DIDN'T LOVE TODAY.

Be Blessed
Deaconess
Pearl Holmes

28 YESTERDAY

Have you watched the dawn fade away,

And the sun's beams make a new day?

Tomorrow is now; To day,

And yesterday is now but yesterday.

Will someone remember because you cast a loving smile their way?

Or will helped to find hope and faith.

Did you stop to hear a crying child's cry turn to laughter and play?

Did you stop to pray, when things did not go your way?

If you did not make someone happy yesterday, there will always be tomorrow....

If you didn't love today.

By: Pearl Holmes

29 THE AUTHOR

This is the day the Lord has made, I hope all is well and Rejoicing in it.

I am Tommie Pearl Holmes. I was born in Cataula Ga., on December Twenty-Fifth Nineteen Twenty from the parents of Janie Iola and Jacob Ward. My family moved to Columbus Ga. When I was three years old, I went to fifth Avenue Grade School. I started there in the second grade because I was taught at home by my mother who was a supply teacher. I also had two aunts who were teachers.

I attended Spencer Vocational High School in Columbus, Ga, where I majored in Home Economics and Nursing. I also attended Jamaica Vocational High School of Jamaica New York, where I continued my Training for Practical Nursing.

One of my aunts was the Principal of East Highland High School. I had many talented helpful members in my family who taught me and helped me along, by editing my writing and encouraging me to take up writing seriously. The rest is HISTORY.

I worked six years for the state and nine years for The City Of New York, and also eighteen years at Star Registry for Nurses in Brooklyn, New York.

I was a member of Jackson Memorial AMEZ Church. I transferred from Jackson to Calvary AMEZ Church in Jamaica, New York, because it was more convenient for me to reach.

My present Pastor is Rev. Dr. E. Alex Brower of Calvary Baptist Church, New York.

30 ABOUT THE AUTHOR

I got nothing but love for my Grandma, but unfortunately she was not able to realize it. She got taken advantage of by certain individuals which I care not to mention and her Alzheimer's disease took effect on her.

Praise her, praise her soul because she just was to slick for herself and ended with the witches that she trusted (If the shoe fits, then wear it). They turn on everybody, so why not turn on her to their advantage. Yea, right!

All photographs were done my Mother Pearl's husband Henry M. Holmes, my grandfather. He was one of the greatest unrecognized painters there was. I once said "Why you don't sell your paintings?" His reply was, "I love doing what I do so I just paint and paint for fun." This is what grandpa Holmes did. Paint for fun. This is his homage. This is for grandpa and grandma. My their spirits last forever in this book.

Henry Holmes
Http://henrysarts.weebly.com

www.ingramcontent.com/pod-product-compliance
Lightning Source LLC
Chambersburg PA
CBHW041529090426

42738CB00035B/4